Tight ends, wide receivers, linebackers, flanker backs, blitzes, "T" formations — these are just a few of the terms that make up the colorful and sometimes confusing language of present-day football. Young football fans and players will find in this book the most up-to-date football terms — professional and collegiate — clearly explained in an easy-to-read dictionary format. Over 130 humorous drawings expand and illustrate the text.

Concise definitions of hand signals, plays, penalties, positions, and much more will help resolve disputes during backyard scrimmages, televised games, and Monday-morning-quarterbacking sessions.

Author Olgin includes a brief history of the game and an extensive section on the greatest football players of all time.

ILLUSTRATED FOOTBALL DICTIONARY FOR YOUNG PEOPLE

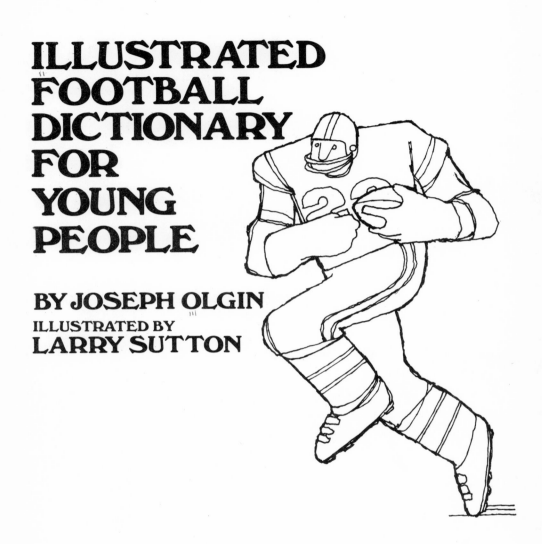

BY JOSEPH OLGIN

ILLUSTRATED BY
LARRY SUTTON

HARVEY HOUSE
New York, New York

To my grandson, Lance, who loves football

Copyright © 1975 Harvey House

All rights reserved, including
the right to reproduce this book
or portions thereof in any form.

Library of Congress Catalog Card Number 74-82014
Manufactured in the United States of America
ISBN 0-8178-5181-X, Trade Edition. ISBN 0-8178-5182-8, Library Edition.

Harvey House, New York, New York

Foreword

Organized football began in the United States in 1869 when Princeton met Rutgers in the first collegiate contest. Its counterparts in Europe, rugby and soccer, have a more ancient background. They are said to have started when victorious warriors kicked the skulls of their victims all over the fields.

After the Rutgers-Princeton challenge, other colleges adopted the game and it spread quickly to high schools. College and high school football soon became recognized as an exciting, popular spectator sport. Professional football began with a shaky start in the early 1900's. Now it overshadows the collegiate and high school game.

Football has changed greatly over the years. Originally, team members played both offensive and defensive positions. Then football became a platoon game with offensive and defensive specialists. These developed, still later, into more individualized specialists such as place kickers, kickoff artists, punters, entire kickoff teams, "suicide" teams sent in to prevent long runbacks on kickoffs and punts, and teams put in solely for place kicking and points after touchdowns.

The language of the game has increased and changed as football evolved in new directions. Audiences began to hear of tight ends, wide receivers, linebackers, flanker backs, blitzes, "T" formations, split "T" formations, dumping the quarterback, etc.

This dictionary has incorporated the football terms used in America today by players, coaches, fans and broadcasters. Outdated and regional terms have been omitted.

A

Advance to the two-yard line — The ball carrier runs to the two-yard line before he is stopped, tackled, or forced out of bounds.

All-American Team — An offensive and defensive team selected yearly by sportswriters from all parts of the country. It is made up of the best college players who performed during the season.

All-Professional Team — Each year coaches and sportswriters pick the best offensive and defensive team from the ranks of professional players in the National Football League and American Football Conference.

Average on the return — The average yardage the ball carrier gains returning kicks or kickoffs. Example: if the ball carrier returns one kick twenty yards, another five yards, and another twenty-five yards, he would have gained fifty yards in three returns. Dividing fifty by three, his average return is 16⅔ yards.

B

Backfield — The backfield typically consists of the quarterback, left halfback, right halfback, and fullback.

Backfield in motion — One or more offensive backs moving before the ball is snapped. The penalty is five yards.

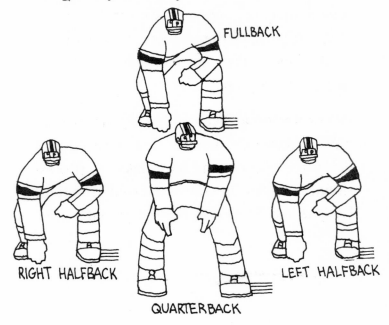

FULLBACK

RIGHT HALFBACK

QUARTERBACK

LEFT HALFBACK

Backward spin — The quarterback takes the snap from center, makes a half turn with his back to the line, then either hands off or fakes a handoff, and runs laterally to the line. He may also drop back and throw a forward pass.

Balanced line — An equal number of players on either side of the center on the offensive line. The right guard, tackle, and end are on the right side of the center. The left guard, tackle, and end are on the left side of the center in a seven-man line.

 END   R.TACKLE   R.GUARD   CENTER   L.GUARD   L.TACKLE   L.END

Ball control — When a team holds the ball for a series of downs, it is called ball control. Many teams plan to hold possession of the ball as their main game plan, with the idea that the other team cannot score while they have possession of the ball, excluding the possibility of a safety.

11

Big hole in the line — The offensive line charges forward and blocks the defensive linemen to either side, thus creating an opening in the defensive line.

Blind pass — The center snaps the ball back without watching its flight.

Blind side tackle — A member of a defensive team hits the ball carrier or the quarterback from behind or from the side, where he can't see the tackler.

Blitz — The defensive linebackers and line-men pour through the line to dump the quarterback or the ball carrier.

BALL CARRIER

Blocked kick — The defensive team crashes through and blocks a punt or a place kick.

Blocking — The offensive players protect the ball carrier by throwing their bodies across the defensive players' bodies to enable the runner to gain ground.

13

Block out front — An offensive lineman pulls out of the line and runs interference for the runner either off tackle or around the end.

Bomb — The quarterback heaves a forward pass for a substantial gain or a touchdown.

Bootleg — This is a deceptive play in which the quarterback fakes a handoff to one of the backs, then hides the ball behind his right or left hip and runs himself around the defensive end.

Box defense — A defensive line of seven men, with two linebackers behind it and two halfbacks farther back, box formation (7-2-2). The offensive line is balanced. The wingback is about two yards behind the end. The blocking back is two yards behind the corresponding guard. The other two backs are two yards farther back from the blocking back, flanking him.

Breakaway runner — A fast, tricky runner, such as O. J. Simpson of the Buffalo Bills, who can break away from opponents in the open field for long gains or touchdowns.

Broken field run — The ball carrier turns, twists and side-steps as he evades tacklers in the open field.

Buck — The ball carrier plunges directly into the line of scrimmage. It is sometimes called a plunge.

Bump and run — An offensive player, usually an end, bumps into the man trying to block him. He then slides off and runs an evasive pattern to catch a pass.

Burn — The receiver completely baffles and eludes the defender to catch a pass for a long gain or a touchdown.

Buttonhook — Evasive tactic by a pass receiver in which he turns suddenly and takes a step back towards the line in an effort to get clear from the defender and catch a pass.

C

Carry — The ball carrier runs with the ball. This is known as a carry.

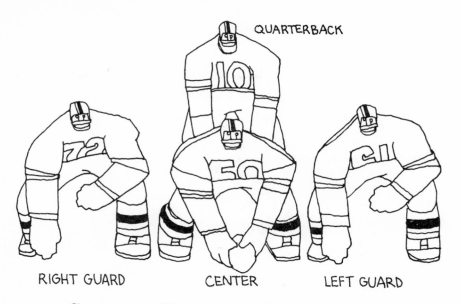

QUARTERBACK

RIGHT GUARD   CENTER   LEFT GUARD

Center — 1. The player in the middle of the offensive line. He snaps the ball back to the quarterback, punter, or the holder for points after touchdowns and field goals. A different center is sometimes used for punts and field goals because of the greater distance the ball has to be snapped. 2. The defensive center plays in the middle of the line and attempts to dump the quarterback or stop the runner from advancing.

Check block — A legal block used to check or hold up an opponent for a moment.

Check play — The quarterback suddenly calls a different play at the line of scrimmage due to a change in the defensive formation.

17

Choice pass — The quarterback takes his choice of several players on a forward pass play rather than being committed to throw to one specified target.

Clipping — A player throws his body across the back of a leg or legs of a player not carrying the ball. This is a personal foul. The penalty is the loss of 15 yards from the point where the infraction took place.

Clothesline tackle — The defensive player tackles the ball carrier with a vicious grab around the neck.

Coaching box — The coaching box is forty yards long and three yards wide. It is located two yards from the sideline. The coach walks up and down in the box following the plays.

Coffin corner — The corners of the field, and the area ten yards or less from the defending team's goal line.

Coming out of the backfield — The offensive back runs out of the backfield either to the left or right side to catch a pass.

Conversion — A score made on a try for an extra point after touchdown by place-kicking or drop-kicking the ball over the bar between the goal posts, or by running the ball or completing a pass into the end zone. In college football, a forward pass or run after a touchdown counts for two points.

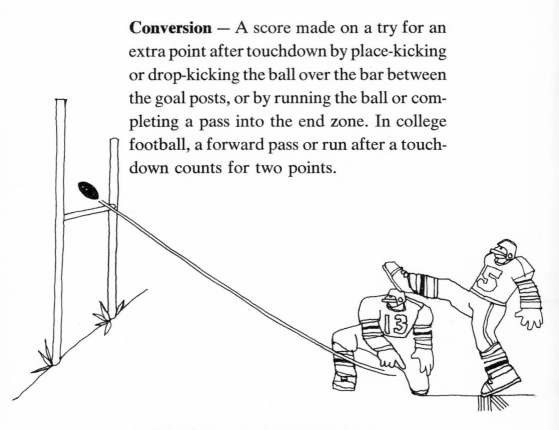

Cornerback — One of the defensive backs who plays either on the left corner or the right corner.

Corner flag — A flag with a flexible staff placed at the inside corners of the four intersections of the goal lines and sidelines. It is useful in determining whether the runner made a touchdown or stepped outside.

20

Cover — Guarding a player or a zone in a defense against a running or passing attack.

Crack-back block — The flanker back lines up three yards wide of the opposing defensive end. Then he "cracks" back into the defensive end at top speed for a crack-back block. Penalty for blocking below the waist is fifteen yards.

Crawling — A runner tries to gain illegal yardage after he is downed, or he tries to crawl a few extra feet after the play has been stopped.

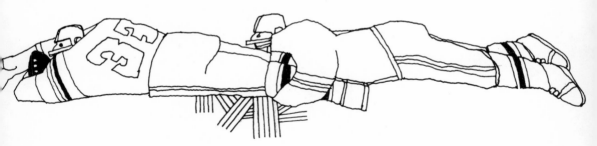

Crisscross — 1. A player catches a punt. He starts towards one sideline and passes the ball back to a teammate headed toward the other sideline. 2. Two eligible pass receivers cross over into a territory diagonally opposite, instead of heading straight downfield.

Cross buck — Two offensive backs crisscross heading towards the line of scrimmage. One fakes receiving the ball from the quarterback, and the other actually takes it and tries to run into the line or around the end for a gain.

Crossbar — The bar beween the goal posts. It is ten feet from the ground.

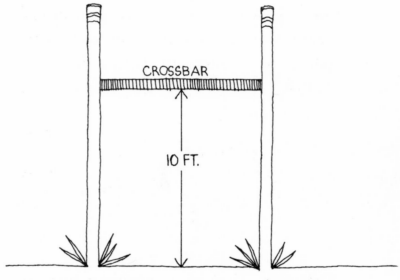

Cross-body block — A player throws his body across an opposing player's body.

Cut back — The ball carrier starts as if to run wide around the end; then he slants back sharply into the line.

D

Dead ball — The ball is not in play, such as in a time-out.

Decision — 1. The quarterback decides on a certain play while in the huddle. 2. The coach sends in a substitute with the play.

QUARTERBACK

Defense — The defensive team attempts to halt the progress and prevent any scoring by the offensive team.

Defensive end — The end who plays on the defensive line when the opponents have the ball.

Defensive holding — Illegal use of the hands and arms by a player whose team does not have possession of the ball. The penalty is five yards from the point where the ball was put in play.

Defensive pass interference — The defensive player illegally interferes with the offensive pass receiver in order to stop him from catching the ball. The pass is then considered as completed by the officials who place it into play where the infraction occurred.

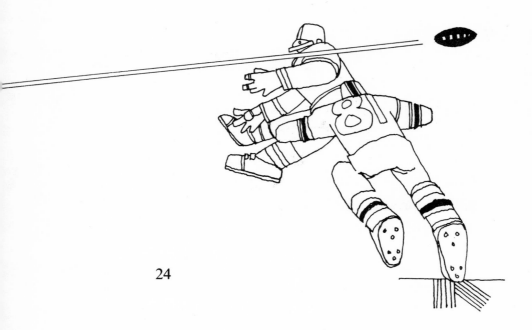

Defensive play — The formation adopted by the defensive team to stop the opponents from gaining ground or scoring a touchdown.

Defensive secondary — The backfield of the defensive team. They can be lined up in a zone defense, or in a man-to-man defense according to the game plan.

Delayed buck — After a series of decoy moves by one back, another back takes the ball from the quarterback and slams into the line.

Delayed pass — A fake pass to one receiver followed by a real pass to another receiver.

Diamond defense — Seven men on the line (7-1-2-1), one linebacker is near center of the line, two halfbacks farther back, and the safety man, still farther back.

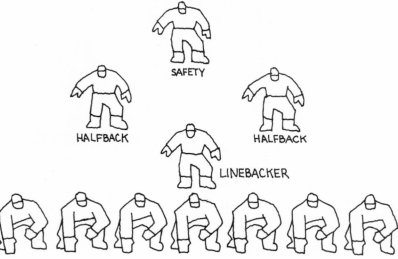

Dive — A headlong plunge into the center of the line.

Double pass — Quarterback flips the ball to another back, who then throws a forward pass.

Double team — 1. Two blockers are assigned to guard a formidable opponent in the line. 2. Two defenders are assigned to stop an outstanding pass receiver or running back.

Double wing — An offensive formation where the quarterback plays directly behind the center. One back plays behind the quarterback, and the other two backs play on either side of the back stationed behind the quarterback.

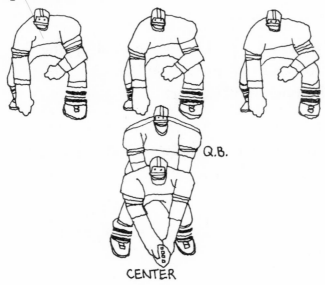

Q.B.

CENTER

Down — One of the four consecutive plays in which the team holding the ball must score or advance the ball a minimum of ten yards in order to keep possession of it.

Down the middle — The quarterback throws the ball to one of his eligible receivers directly over the line of scrimmage.

Draw play — The offensive line allows a lineman or several linemen to come in. The quarterback then hands the ball to a ball carrier who runs through the hole vacated by the defensive lineman, or linemen. Meanwhile, his own linemen are set to give him interference.

Drop kick — A kick made by dropping the football to the ground and kicking it before it rebounds off the turf.

Dying quail — A weak, fluttering forward pass which is so ineffectual that it is intercepted by the defense.

E

End around — The offensive end turns back into his own backfield the instant the center snaps the ball back. He receives the ball from the quarterback and attempts to gain ground by running around the opposite end.

28

End over end — The motion of the ball when it rotates on its axis, the two points whirling in a plane perpendicular to the ground. This usually happens on drop kicks and place kicks. The ball generally travels in a spiral plane on punts and forward passes. Some punters and passes, however, get good results with end-over-end kicks and passes.

End run — The ball carrier attempts to run around the defensive end. He is usually preceded by several blockers.

Ends — The men stationed at the extreme right and left ends of the line.

Ends pinching on the quarterback — The defensive ends, playing wide, crash in on the quarterback from opposite sides.

End zone — The ten-yard area between the goal line and the end of the playing field.

Excessive time-out — A team is allowed four periods of time-out in each half. If the captain requests another time-out, the penalty is five yards, unless it is called to remove an injured player.

F

Fair catch — A back who sees that he cannot advance the ball while fielding a punt can raise his hand a full arm's length above his head to signal a fair catch. No opponent can interfere as he attempts to catch the ball. He can also let the ball go by him, but if it touches any part of his body while bouncing around, it becomes a fumble or a free ball. After a fair catch, the player cannot run with the ball. It is placed down where he caught it.

Fair catch infraction — If the receiver raises his hand to signal a fair catch and is then run into by an opposing player or players, the officials will signal a fair catch infraction. The penalty is fifteen yards from the point of the foul.

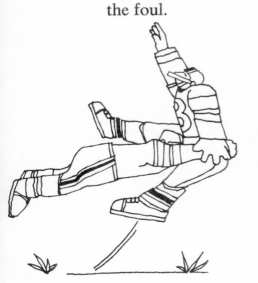

15 YARDS

Fake kick — A player pretends to kick the ball, then he runs with it or throws a forward pass.

False start — A defensive player makes a deliberate feint at starting a play with the intention of drawing his opponents offside. The penalty is five yards from the line of scrimmage.

Far side — The side of the field farthest away from the ball.

Field goal — The offensive team kicks the ball over the crossbar and between the opponent's goal post. It may place-kick or drop-kick the ball. If missed, ball is returned to line of scrimmage or twenty-yard line, whichever is farther from the goal line. A field goal counts three points.

Field judge — The official timekeeper for the game.

Field position — When the receiving team gets the ball on a kickoff or on a punt and advances it at least to their own forty-yard line, they have good field position.

First down — The first play in a series of four. A team must gain ten yards within four plays in order to retain possession of the ball.

First quarter — The first quarter of play begins with the opening kickoff and lasts fifteen playing minutes.

Five-three-two-one defense — There are five players on the line, three linebackers behind them, two halfbacks farther back, and a safety man at the rear.

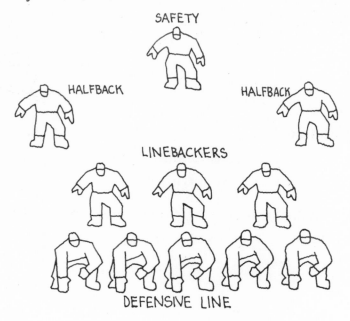

Flag down — The officials throw a colored handkerchief to the ground to indicate a rule infraction.

Flankers — Offensive players stationed at the far ends of the scrimmage line.

Flat pass — A pass thrown straight to the sideline or into the flat zone.

Flat zone — The area on each side of the scrimmage line extending about five yards into the defensive territory.

Flooding a zone — Several receivers running into the same area in a passing attack.

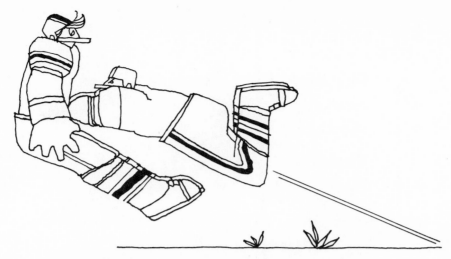

Flying block — A blocker diving or hurling his body through the air at an opponent. A blocker may leave his feet only at the moment of contact. The penalty for the flying block is five yards from the point of the foul.

Football Hall of Fame — An organization established in 1963 in Canton, Ohio, to honor and elect to membership football "greats" — outstanding players, coaches, commissioners, owners, and others who have contributed significantly to the sport. There is also a College Hall of Fame located in New Brunswick, New Jersey, where Rutgers and Princeton played the first collegiate football game in 1869.

Forced out — The ball carrier is pushed or knocked out of bounds.

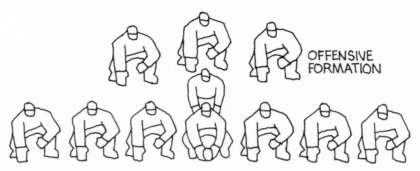

OFFENSIVE
FORMATION

Formation — The line-up of eleven players in offensive or defensive positions.

Forward pass — A pass in which the ball is thrown toward the opponent's goal.

Forward wall — The line is called the forward wall. The line consists of the center, two guards, two tackles and two ends.

36

Four-four-three defense — A defensive alignment consisting of four players on the line, four linebackers, and three backs farther in the rear. It is used mostly when a forward pass is expected.

HALFBACKS

LINEBACKERS

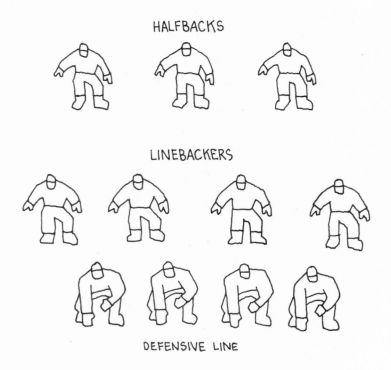

DEFENSIVE LINE

Four points stance — The player crouches with both hands on the ground in front of him. Thus he has contact with the ground at four points, both hands, and both feet.

37

Free kick — The defensive team is restrained from advancing on the kicker beyond a certain line before the ball is actually kicked. The restraining line for the kicking team is a line parallel to the goal line through the most forward part of the ball. For defensive opponents, it is a line parallel to and ten yards in advance of the kicking team's restraining line. A free kick is indicated in the following situations: 1. the kickoff; 2. free kick after a fair catch; 3. free kick after a safety.

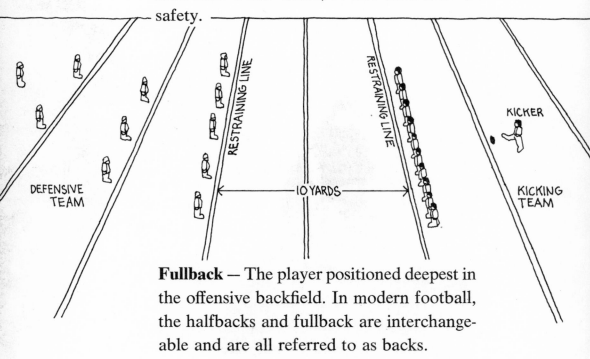

DEFENSIVE TEAM

RESTRAINING LINE

RESTRAINING LINE

KICKER

KICKING TEAM

10 YARDS

Fullback — The player positioned deepest in the offensive backfield. In modern football, the halfbacks and fullback are interchangeable and are all referred to as backs.

Full spinner — A play where a back fakes a hand-off to a teammate when he has taken a half spin and is facing away from the line of scrimmage. He keeps the ball and completes his spin to face the line of scrimmage. He then attempts a run for a gain.

Fumble — A player drops or mishandles the ball, which falls to the ground.

G

Get outside — The ball carrier attempts to run out of bounds to stop the clock.

Getting a block — The ball carrier has one of his teammates block a would-be tackler out of his way so he can get running room. It can also occur in the open field, enabling the ball carrier to make a long gain or a touchdown.

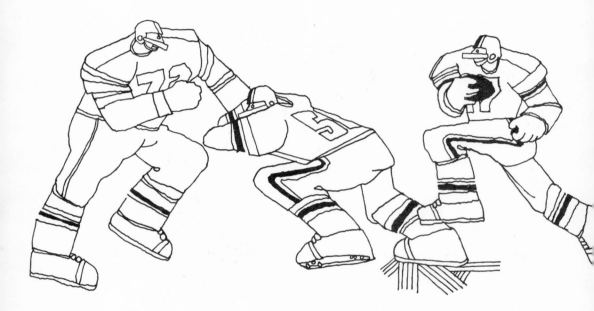

Gets the call — The quarterback in the huddle designates which back is to carry the ball or which receiver is to catch the pass.

Goal line — Lines marking the end of the playing field.

Goal line corner flag — A flag is set in the ground on a rubber pole about two feet high at each corner of the goal lines. The flag bends easily so that game officials can determine if a runner stepped over the sidelines before crossing the goal line.

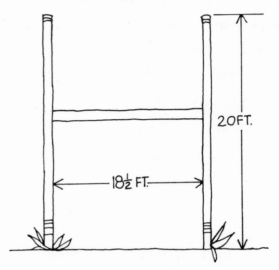

Goal posts — The goal posts are eighteen and a half feet apart and stand twenty feet high. A crossbar is fastened to both goal posts ten feet above the ground. Crossbars can be made of wood, aluminum or steel pipe.

Goal line stand — A defensive team, with its back up against its own goal line, successfully stops the offense from scoring.

41

Grandstand quarterback — A fan who makes a nuisance of himself by second-guessing the quarterback if a play is unsuccessful.

Grounded — An incomplete forward pass that hits the ground.

Guards — Right and left. The players on either side of the center.

H

Half spinner — A back spins halfway around with his back to the line of scrimmage. He then hands the ball to a teammate who attempts to make a gain.

Half time — A fifteen-minute rest period between the second and third quarters. Often marching bands, twirlers and strutters provide colorful entertainment during this period.

42

Hand-off — The offensive quarterback gives the ball to one of his ball carriers.

Hand signals —

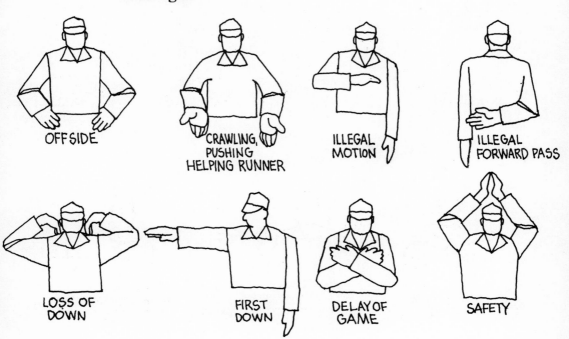

OFFSIDE

CRAWLING, PUSHING HELPING RUNNER

ILLEGAL MOTION

ILLEGAL FORWARD PASS

LOSS OF DOWN

FIRST DOWN

DELAY OF GAME

SAFETY

HOLDING

TOUCHDOWN,
FIELD GOAL

DEAD
BALL

TIME-OUT

INELIGIBLE RECEIVER
DOWNFIELD

PERSONAL
FOUL

ILLEGAL
PROCEDURE

PENALTY REFUSED,
INCOMPLETE PASS,
MISSED GOAL

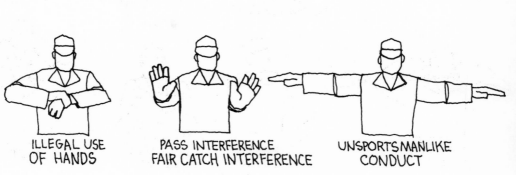

ILLEGAL USE
OF HANDS

PASS INTERFERENCE
FAIR CATCH INTERFERENCE

UNSPORTSMANLIKE
CONDUCT

Hash lines — The two short lines intersecting each five-yard line. They divide the width of the field into three equal parts. There are two hash lines in each of the yard lines.

Head block — A blocker drives his head into the opponent he is blocking.

Head linesman — The official, who, with his assistants, marks the progress of the ball.

Hidden ball — The runner uses a spinner, or a reverse, in which the ball is hidden from the defensive players. Example: the quarterback spins and hides the ball behind his hip.

Hiding the ball on the hip — The offensive quarterback fakes a hand-off to one of his backs. Instead, he hides the ball on his hip and runs with it himself or throws a pass.

Hit by the end — The defensive end crashes in on the quarterback or the ball carrier.

Hits fifty percent of his passes — The offensive quarterback successfully completes half of his pass attempts.

Holding — A player grabs his opponent with his hands to block him or impede his progress. Either defensive or offensive holding can be penalized. For offensive holding, the penalty is fifteen yards (college), ten yards (NFL). For defensive holding, it is five yards.

QUARTERBACK

Huddle — Players form into a tight circle behind the line or the quarterback stands facing his ten teammates in order to instruct them on the next play.

Hurdling — An attempt by the ball carrier to jump over a defensive player who is in his way. Current rules state that the defensive player being hurdled by the ball carrier must have at least one knee on the ground.

I

Illegal delay — In high school and college football, a quarterback must get the play off in twenty-five seconds. In professional football, the time is thirty seconds. Otherwise the official will call an illegal delay, and a five yard penalty is incurred. Substitutions must be made with no delay.

Illegal pass — 1. The quarterback runs past the line of scrimmage before releasing the ball. 2. The quarterback completes a pass to an ineligible receiver downfield.

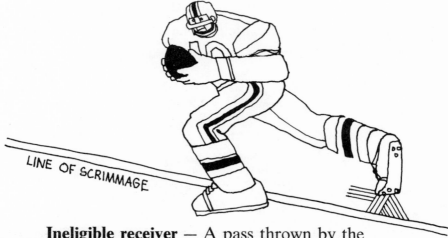

LINE OF SCRIMMAGE

Ineligible receiver — A pass thrown by the quarterback to a guard, tackle, or center downfield.

Illegal shift — Occurs when all eleven offensive players fail to come to a full stop for at least one second before the ball is snapped. The penalty is five yards.

Illegal use of hands — Holding or pushing by offensive players. The penalty is fifteen yards (college), ten yards (NFL).

Incomplete pass — A forward pass which has not been caught and falls to the ground.

Inside fake — The ball carrier makes a feint to the inside of the line and then runs to the outside.

Inside option — An option play where the quarterback plans to go through the line of scrimmage, anywhere within the bounds of the two offensive ends, depending upon where the hole develops.

Interception — A defending player catches a pass intended for an offensive player.

Interference — 1. Illegally preventing a pass receiver from catching the ball. 2. The pass receiver illegally interferes with the defensive player by pushing or tripping him. 3. Players who block for the ball carrier are running interference for him.

Interference call — When a defensive player interferes with an opponent by holding, pushing, or tripping him, the official will call it a completed pass. When the offensive player does the same to the defensive player in order to catch a pass, the officials will rule the pass incomplete even if the receiver catches the ball.

In the open — A runner breaks through and is free of all tacklers.

Intentional grounding — The quarterback deliberately throws the ball down to prevent being tackled for a loss. The penalty is five yards.

In touch — The status of the ball crossing either goal line. It can become dead behind the goal line, or else become a touchdown, safety, touchback, or field goal.

J

Jump pass — The passer jumps in the air and throws the ball while both feet are off the ground.

K

Keep — The quarterback fakes a hand-off, but keeps the ball.

Key — A defensive player concentrates on watching an offensive player to see if his actions can tip off or "key" the coming play.

Kick from scrimmage — A kick can be made by a punt, place kick, or drop kick from behind the scrimmage line. No member of the kicking team may cross the line of scrimmage until the ball is kicked: nor may he recover the ball until it touches an opponent. The receiving team may recover the ball, run with it, pass backward, or kick the ball.

Kicking a free ball — Kicking or attempting to kick a free ball is an infraction of the rules. The penalty is loss of the ball to the other team, unless it is obviously an accident. If it is done in the end zone, it is a touchdown or a safety, depending upon which team committed the foul.

Kicking lane — A space that is kept free from opponents by the kicker's teammates so that the kicker may safely complete his kick.

Kicking unit — Special players sent in when a team wishes to punt, try for a field goal, or make a conversion after a touchdown.

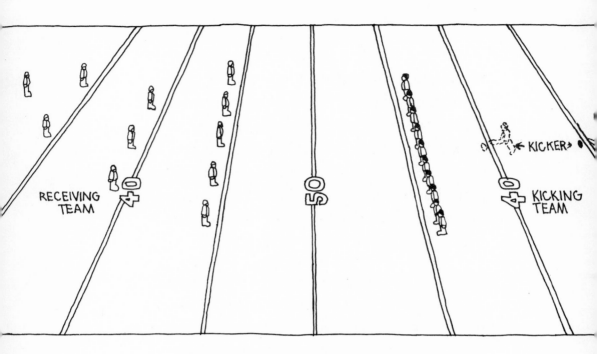

RECEIVING TEAM

KICKER

KICKING TEAM

Kickoff — The beginning play of the game. A place kick from the forty-yard line (35-yard line, NFL) of the kicking team that puts the ball in play at the beginning of each half or after a field goal or a touchdown.

Kickoff return — The runback made by a player who catches the kickoff either on the field or in the end zone.

Kickoff return team — Special players who are sent in before the other team kicks off.

Kick return — The runback made by a player who catches a punt.

54

OUT OF BOUNDS

Kill the clock — During the last few minutes of a game, the players of a team needing to conserve time attempt to get out of bounds while running or catching a pass in order to stop the clock.

Knife through — The ball carrier slashes through the slightest opening in the line.

L

Lateral pass — The ball is passed sideways or laterally across the field from one player to another.

Lead — 1. A player blocks in front of the runner or leads him. 2. When the quarterback throws the ball in front of the receiver, it is called leading the receiver.

Lead the charge — The blocker who runs in front of the ball carrier leads the charge.

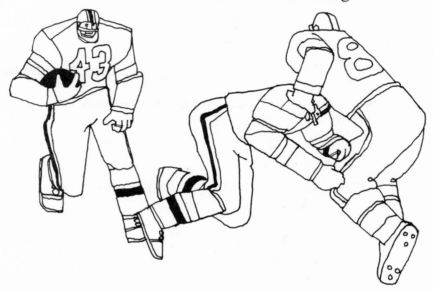

Leading the play — The blockers who run in front of the ball carrier, providing him interference.

Legal delay — A delay that is created by the captain requesting a time-out for suspension of play, to bring in substitutes, or to remove an injured player.

56

Linebackers — The players positioned behind the linemen in a defensive formation. They are the right linebacker, the middle linebacker, and the left linebacker, depending upon which part of the defensive line they stand behind.

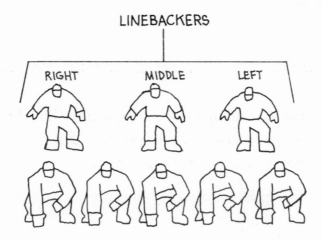

Linemen — Players in the forward offensive or defensive line — guards, tackles, centers, and ends.

Linesmen — The assistant officials who mark the distances gained and lost in the progress of play and determine where the ball goes out of bounds.

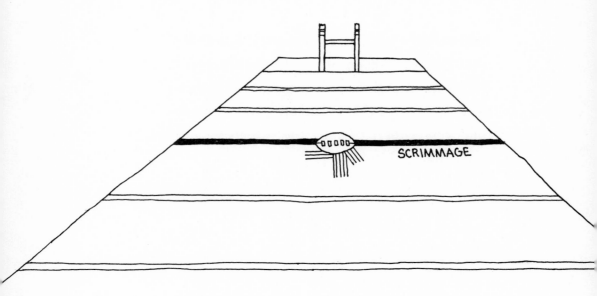

Line of scrimmage — An imaginary line that runs parallel to the goal posts. It denotes the starting position for the next play.

Long gain — Any play that results in a substantial advance.

Looping — A defensive maneuver which occurs when the linemen step laterally before charging forward, in an attempt to confuse the offensive linemen. Meanwhile, the linebackers loop in the opposite direction.

Loose — A formation where the players are relatively far apart from one another with the ends playing very wide.

58

Loose ball — 1. The ball carrier or pass receiver fumbles the ball. 2. A player receiving a punt drops the ball. Any player can fall on it and gain possession except in the case of a fumbled pass.

M

Making the stop — The defensive player who tackles or blocks the ball carrier and brings him down.

Marker down — An official throws his colored flag on the ground when he sees an infraction of the rules or a foul committed. The flag is dropped at the point of infraction.

MIDDLE
GUARD

Middle guard — The lineman on the defensive line who plays head-up (directly opposite) on the center.

Middle linebacker — The defensive linebacker who plays in the middle of the line.

Midfield — The fifty-yard line.

Mousetrap—The defensive player is allowed to move unhindered through the offensive line; then he is blocked from the side.

Muff — An unsuccessful attempt to catch a ball. Example: a safety back tries to catch a punt; instead he muffs it, or fumbles it, to the ground.

N

Naked reverse — All the interference on the offensive team moves to one side. The ball carrier then runs in the opposite direction without any blockers to run interference for him.

60

Near side — The side of the field nearest to the sideline where the offensive team puts the ball in play.

Necktie tackle — A defensive player grabs the ball carrier around the neck and knocks him to the ground.

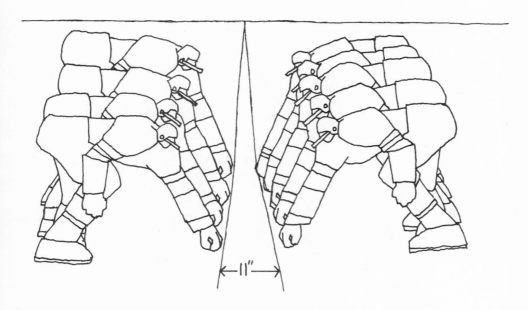

Neutral zone — The space between the lines of scrimmage of the two teams. It extends across the field. It measures eleven to eleven-and-a-quarter inches, or the length of the football from point-to-point.

Non-cadence — A deceptive maneuver in which the quarterback barks the signals and avoids a definite rhythm. He is trying to mislead the defense and pull one or more of them offside.

No return — A player who catches a punt or a kickoff is dropped in his tracks for no gain.

O

Offense — The team possessing the ball and trying to advance it.

Offensive guard — The guard either to the right or left of the center on the offensive team.

Offensive holding — An offensive player grabs or holds a defensive player. The penalty is fifteen yards (college), ten yards (NFL).

Offensive pass interference — Pushing or tripping a defensive player in order to catch a pass. The penalty is an incomplete pass if the offensive player catches the ball.

Offside — Occurs when any part of a player's body is ahead of the ball, his line of scrimmage, or the restraining line immediately before the ball is put into play. The penalty is five yards.

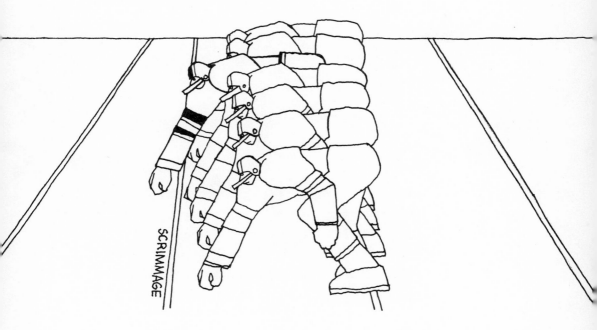

SCRIMMAGE

Off tackle — The offensive back runs near or just outside the position held by the offensive tackle. This is one of football's most frequently used running plays.

Onside — All players are legally in correct position to start a play or a kickoff.

Onside kickoff — When the kicking team on a kickoff attempts to recover the ball after it has gone at least ten yards, it is called an onside kickoff.

On target — The quarterback hits the man or the spot he is throwing to.

Open field — The field behind the defensive line of scrimmage. It is called the open field because the defensive backs are spaced farther apart and are not as closely packed as in the line.

Option play — The quarterback is free to choose whether to pass, run, or hand off the ball.

Optional pass — The passer has more than one receiver who is ready to catch the ball, or the passer may run with it.

Out of bounds — A ball is out of bounds when it goes out of the playing area. It is then called a dead ball and must be put back into play by the officials. A player is out of bounds if he runs or steps out of the marked playing area.

P

Pay dirt — The end zones where the touchdowns are made.

Penalty — A disadvantage imposed upon a team for infraction of the rules.

Perfect strike — A sharp, quick pass thrown by the quarterback to a receiver.

Personal foul — An illegally rough play created by striking, kneeing, or kicking an opponent, for roughing the kicker, piling on, hurdling illegally, unnecessary roughness, clipping, roughing the passer, or pulling on the face mask. The penalty for most personal fouls is fifteen yards.

Piling up on the thirty — A pile-up of players caused by the defensive team stopping a line play on the thirty-yard line.

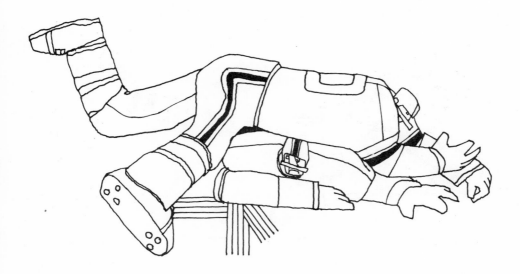

Piling on — This can occur in two ways: 1. illegally falling on a downed player other than the ball carrier; 2. piling on the ball carrier after the ball is ruled dead. This is considered unsportsmanlike conduct. The penalty is fifteen yards. If the foul is flagrant, the official can throw the offending player out of the game.

Pitch out — The quarterback tosses a quick, short, underhand pass to either halfback or the fullback, who then attempts to run wide around the end.

Place kick — A play for scoring a field goal for three points where the ball is kicked from a fixed position on the ground and held by a teammate of the kicker. It is never elevated more than one inch. A regulation tee may be used.

68

Placer — The player who kneels or holds the ball for the place kicker.

Platoon — There are two types of platoons in football: the players who play on the offense; and those who play on the defense.

Players' bench — Benches on each side of the field, near the fifty-yard line and inside the coaching box area, for team members.

50

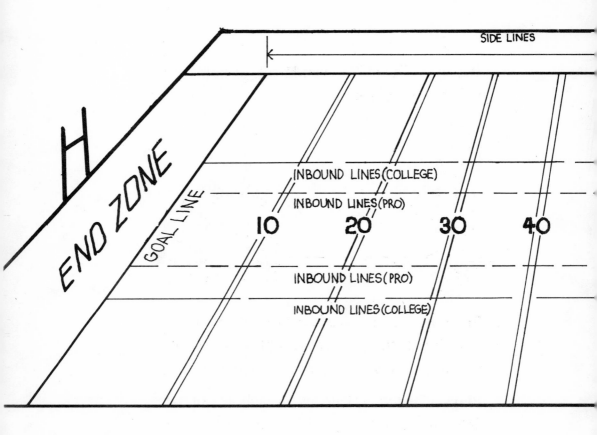

END ZONE

GOAL LINE

INBOUND LINES (COLLEGE)

INBOUND LINES (PRO)

10   20   30   40

INBOUND LINES (PRO)

INBOUND LINES (COLLEGE)

Playing field — The playing field is 300 feet long and 160 feet wide. Goal posts stand at each end. An extra ten yards, known as end zones, are added to each end of the field. The goal posts are located ten yards back of the goal line. White lines mark every five yards across the width of the field. Starting at

70

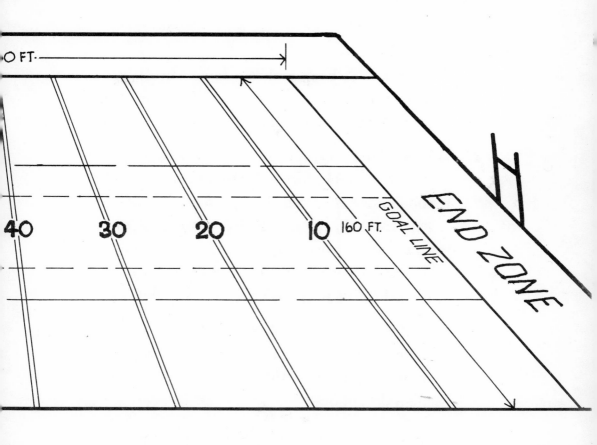

the fifty-yard line, which is the center of the
field, the cross-lines are numbered every ten
yards. The numbers read, 50, 40, 30, 20, 10,
on each side of the field. Inside of both sidelines, and running parallel to them, are the
inbound lines. They run the length of the
field.

71

Plunge — A back makes a quick thrust or dive into the line near its center. This is most often done by the fullback.

Point after touchdown — A scoring place kick, drop kick, forward pass or run after a touchdown is scored. In high school or college football, a successful forward pass or run scores two points, while a kick scores one point. In professional football, only a place kick or drop kick scores one point.

Power play — A play in which all supporting offensive players concentrate their strength in one given area without attempting to create a deception.

Pressure on the quarterback — The defensive linemen or linebackers crash in on the quarterback.

Protection — Guarding a particular player or a zone from the opponents.

Pulled hamstring — A painful condition in which the large muscles behind the thigh become so strained or pulled that the player usually must leave the game.

Pulling the face mask — Grabbing the face mask of an opponent is an illegal move, and can cause serious injury. The penalty is five or fifteen yards, depending upon whether the referee judges it intentional or unintentional.

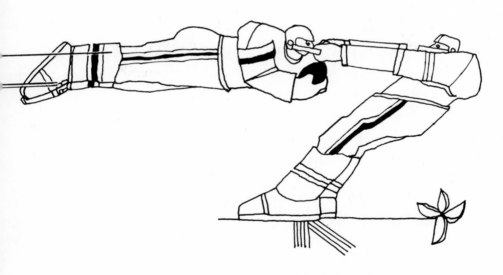

Punt — The player holds the ball in his hand, drops it, and then kicks it before it touches the ground.

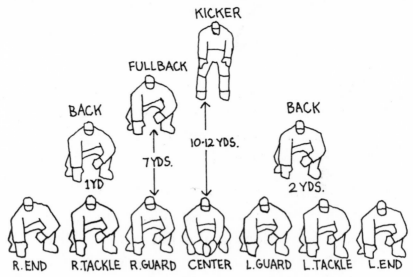

KICKER

FULLBACK

BACK

BACK

10-12 YDS.

7 YDS.

1 YD

2 YDS.

R. END R. TACKLE R. GUARD CENTER L. GUARD L. TACKLE L. END

Punt formation — The kicker is ten to twelve yards behind the center. One back plays about one yard behind the offensive right tackle. The fullback is usually seven yards behind the offensive right guard. The other back places himself two yards behind the point midway between the offensive left guard and left tackle. In a short punt formation, the kicker is only five to seven yards behind the center.

Punt return — An opposing player catches and returns the punt.

Punting team — Specialists who are sent in when a punt is called for.

Pushing — Deliberate pushing incurs a penalty of fifteen yards.

74

Q

Quarter — One of four fifteen-minute periods of actual playing time.

Quarterback — The player whose position is directly behind the center and who generally calls the signals and does the passing. He is responsible for selecting the plays and making the team move the ball.

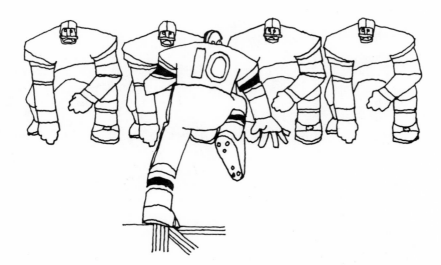

Quarterback sneak — A play where the quarterback keeps the ball instead of passing it or handing it off to a back. He attempts to run or sneak through the center of the line.

Quick kick—A surprise maneuver intended to kick the ball over the defensive safety's head. Usually the punt is made from a short distance behind the line from a formation that indicated a running or passing play. This is generally done on a third down, long yardage situation.

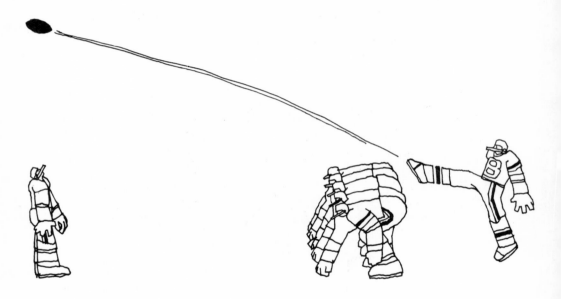

Quick opening — A play designed to take advantage of a momentary opening in the defensive line before the opponents can close it. This is a feature of the "T" formation.

R

Reception — When a receiver catches a pass.

Recovered kick — A ball legally recovered by a member of the kicking team. It must first touch one of the opponents. It cannot be advanced unless it was a kick from scrimmage which failed to cross the scrimmage line.

Red dog — The defensive linebackers crash into the offensive backfield before the offensive play can get going.

Referee — The game's chief official. He is positioned behind the offensive team.

OFFENSIVE TEAM

Restraining line — A line parallel to the goal line through the most forward point from which the ball may be kicked. It may not be passed before the ball is put into play on a free kick. The opponent's restraining line is parallel to and ten yards in front of the kicking team's restraining line.

Reverse — A back starts in one direction and then hands or passes the ball to a teammate running in another direction. This puts the play through the opposite side of the line from what the defense expected. A deep reverse occurs when the ball carrier runs wide around the opposite end from where the defense expected the play to go.

Reverse cross-body block — A head-on shoulder block is feinted. The blocker then reverses his position and blocks with his hip and legs while changing his head position to point in the direction he just came from.

Rifles the ball — A quarterback throws a quick, hard pass to a receiver.

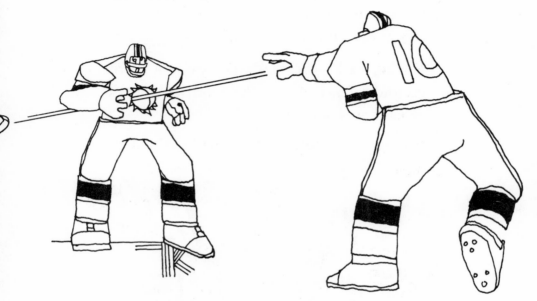

Roll out — A quarterback runs out of his protective pocket of blockers either to pass or run.

Rookie — A young or inexperienced player trying out for the team for the first time.

Roughing the kicker — Slamming or crashing into a player who kicks from behind his own scrimmage line. The penalty is fifteen yards and an automatic first down. If the act is flagrant, the guilty player may be disqualified, that is, thrown out of the game.

Roughing the passer — Crashing into the passer after he has thrown the ball. The penalty is the same as for roughing the kicker.

Roving back — A back who covers a lot of ground defensively. In other words, he moves around or roves.

Ruling — The decision that an official makes on a play.

Runner has daylight — A ball carrier breaks into the clear or sees a wide hole in the line.

Running back — The offensive back who carries the ball.

Running pass — The quarterback fakes a run, then suddenly, while in motion, throws a pass to a receiver.

Run wide — The back runs around the end of the line of scrimmage before he attempts to move ahead.

Rushing — 1. A defensive player charges in to attempt to block a tackle. 2. A back running with the ball through the line is also rushing.

Rushing the passer — Forcing the passer to throw the ball before he is ready.

S

Sacked — The defensive players tackle the quarterback before he can get a pass or a play off.

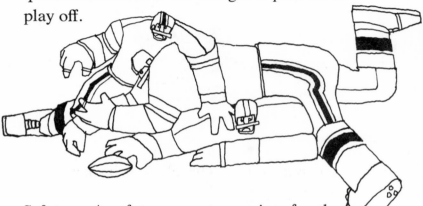

Safety — A safety scores two points for the opposing team and occurs when a ball carrier for the offensive team is tackled in his own end zone or downs the ball there, or when the ball goes out of bounds on a fumble after being in possession of the offensive player in or over the end zone.

Safety blitz — Occurs when a safety leaves his post at the rear of the defense and red-dogs (attacks) the quarterback.

Safety man — The player on the defense who lines up farthest behind the line of scrimmage. His duties are to stop ball carriers who have broken into the open field, intercept or block passes, and receive kicks.

Scatback — A fast, elusive back who is unusually small and light, but tremendously fast and tricky.

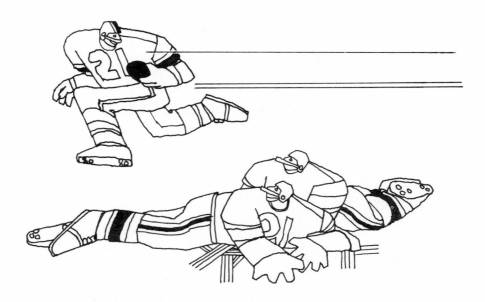

Screen pass — The offensive linemen let their opponents through. The quarterback throws a short pass over the opposing linemen's heads to an eligible receiver.

Scout — 1. A man assigned to figure out or "scout" the upcoming opponent's strategy and tactics before a scheduled game. 2. A man assigned by a college or professional team to locate talented players for his team.

Scrimmage — 1. The action that takes place between opposing teams from the instant the ball is put in motion until it is declared dead. 2. A practice session running through plays, blocking and tackling, running or catching passes.

OFFENSIVE TEAM

SCRIMMAGE LINE

Scrimmage line — An imaginary line parallel to the goal line. It passes through the point of the ball nearest to a given team's goal line. A least seven men of the offensive team must be on it when the ball is snapped. Defensive team players need not be on the scrimmage line.

Scoring drive — A scoring drive is the number of plays it takes for a team to score a touchdown.

Scoreboard — Usually located at one end of the stadium, the scoreboard posts the quarter, the score, the down, the number of yards needed for a first down, and the amount of playing time left in each quarter.

Scrambler — A quarterback who does not stay in the protective pocket and who is a threat in the running game, too.

Scrub — A substitute or member of the second team.

SCRUB

1ST TEAM MEMBER

Secondary — The cornerbacks, linebackers, and the safety man who line up behind the line of scrimmage on defense. Their job is to tackle ball carriers who have passed the scrimmage line, to break up forward passes, and to receive kicks.

Second down and nine — If a team gains only one yard on the first down, it must gain nine yards in the three remaining downs in order to retain possession of the ball.

Second effort — The extra yardage a tackled runner gains by turning on an extra burst of energy to eke out an extra yard or two.

Shakeoff — A ball carrier tears free from a defensive player by shaking him off

Shift — To change offensive or defensive positions before the ball is snapped.

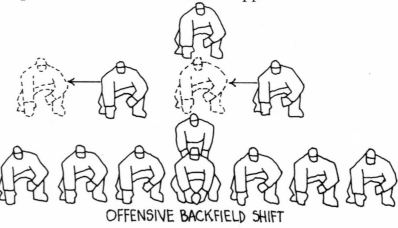

OFFENSIVE BACKFIELD SHIFT

Shoestring tackle — A tackle made around the ankles.

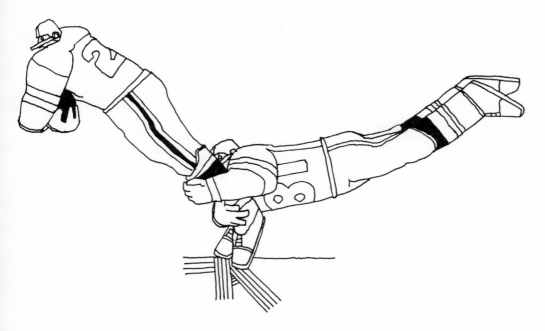

Shooting the gap — Defensive linebackers crashing straight into the offensive backfield through an opening left by offensive blockers.

Shovel pass — The quarterback throws an underhand pass to a back behind or near the scrimmage line.

Shutout — When a team is held scoreless.

Sidelines — The lengthwise boundary lines of the playing field.

Signals — The numbers called by the quarterback before the ball is snapped to indicate the play to be used.

Single wingback — An offensive formation which employs a balanced or unbalanced line. One wingback is stationed about a yard behind the offensive end. He either flanks him, stays inside him, or directly behind him.

WINGBACK

Skirt — The ball carrier runs around the defensive end.

90

Skull practice — Lectures on team strategy by the coach illustrated with diagrams drawn on a blackboard.

Slanting charge — The defensive players charge at their opponents at an angle, sometimes diagonally opposite.

Slant play — A play that does not head directly into the line but rather slants, or angles off, as in an off-tackle play.

Slotback — The back who moves into the ball carrier's spot after a shift.

91

15 YARDS

Slugging — Hitting an opponent with the fist or forearm. It is a personal foul carrying a fifteen-yard penalty.

Snap from center — 1. The center passes the ball between his legs to the quarterback. 2. He can also snap the ball back to a place kicker or punter.

Special teams — In today's highly specialized games, there are special teams for punting, place kicking, kickoff, and punt returns.

Spilled — The ball carrier is tackled to the ground, or spilled.

Spinner — The quarterback receives the ball from the center. He rotates or spins behind the line. He may hand off the ball to a team-mate or he may spin all the way around and keep the ball.

Spin-out pass — The quarterback spins around before he throws a pass.

Split buck — A fake cross buck or a fake reverse.

Split end — An end who splits off from the line and plays wide.

Split line — An offensive line with wide spaces between the players.

R.END   R.TACKLE   R.GUARD   CENTER   L.GUARD   L.TACKLE   L.END

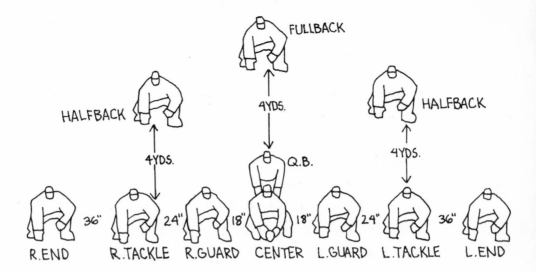

FULLBACK

HALFBACK

4YDS.

4YDS.

Q.B.

4YDS.

HALFBACK

36" 24" 18" 18" 24" 36"

R.END   R.TACKLE   R.GUARD   CENTER   L.GUARD   L.TACKLE   L.END

Split "T"— In the "T" offense, the guards are split about eighteen inches from the center, tackles are split twenty-four inches from the guards, ends are split thirty-six inches from the tackle, the two halfbacks are four yards behind the tackles, positioned on their inside hip, and the fullback, four yards behind the quarterback.

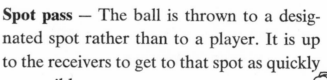

Spot pass — The ball is thrown to a designated spot rather than to a player. It is up to the receivers to get to that spot as quickly as possible.

Spread formation — An offensive alignment where many players spread out laterally. The ends and some of the backs are off a great distance from the center.

Start the clock — After a time-out, the clock is started as play is resumed.

Stationary block — A block without a charge forward. A stationary tackle is one where the tackler waits to see where the ball carrier is going. Then he follows the play.

Statistics — Many papers give a statistical rundown of important games so their readers will understand more clearly what happened. The following is a statistical rundown of a game in which the Dallas Cowboys were defeated by the Washington Redskins 26-3.

	COWBOYS	REDSKINS
First Downs	8	16
Rushing yards	21-96	44-122
Passing yards	73	194
Return yards	49	10
Passes	9-21-0	14-18-0
Punts	7-43	4-36
Fumbles Lost	1-1	2-1
Penalties yards	4-30	4-38

Other statistical rundowns go into greater detail, such as this game in which the Miami Dolphins beat the Pittsburgh Steelers 21-17.

YARDSTICK		
	PITTSBURGH	DOLPHINS
Total First Downs	13	19
First Downs Rushing	6	11
First Downs Passing	6	6
First Downs by Penalty	1	2
Total Offensive Yards	250	314
Total Offensive Plays	48	65
Average Gain per Offensive Play	5.2	4.8
Net Rushing Yards	128	193
Average Gain Rushing Play	4.9	3.9
Net Passing Yards	122	121
Gross Yards Gained Passing	137	121
Yards Lost Attempting to Pass	2-15	0-0
Pass Attempts Intercepted	20-10-2	16-10-1
Average Gain per Pass Play	5.5	7.6
Punts Number and Average	4-51.3	4-35.5
Fumbles Number and Lost	2-0	0-0
Penalties Number and Yards	4-30	2-20
Total Return Yards	118	34
Number and Yards Punt Returns	1.5	0.0
Number and Yards Kickoff Returns	3-85	1-23
Number and Yards Interception Returns	1-28	2-11
Number and Yards Miscellaneous Returns	0	0

97

Statue of Liberty — A trick play where the quarterback holds the ball behind his head as if to throw a pass. A teammate runs behind him, grabs the ball, and runs with it.

Staying in the air — The quarterback throws passes frequently to gain yardage.

Staying on the ground — The quarterback calls mostly running plays to gain yardage.

Staying in the pocket — The quarterback stays in the protective defensive pocket and does not run out of it while passing.

Stiff arm — The legal use of the arm and hand by the ball carrier to ward off a would-be tackler.

Stopped on the play — The ball carrier is stopped without a gain or is thrown for a loss.

Straight buck — A smash straight into the line by a running back.

Stripping — A defensive player upsets the interference, allowing his teammates a better chance to tackle the unprotected ball carrier.

Strong safety — The safety plays on either the right or left side, wherever the offense has amassed its strength.

Strong side — The side of the unbalanced line which has the most players on it.

Stutter step — Many fast, elusive backs use several sharp, quick steps in place to deceive tacklers.

Submarining — The defensive lineman charges forward and dives beneath the knees of his opponent before he pushes up.

Sudden death — An added fifteen-minute period when score is tied. In championship games, contest continues until a team scores.

Sweep play — The player receiving the snap, or handoff, attempts to carry the ball around the defensive end position.

Swivel-hipped — An elusive back, capable through hip control, of changing directions abruptly to shake off tacklers.

Super Bowl — The Super Bowl is the final championship game of professional football. Held annually, it pits the winner of the American Football Conference against the winner of the National Football Conference to determine the year's championship team. It is comparable to The World Series in baseball and The Stanley Cup in hockey.

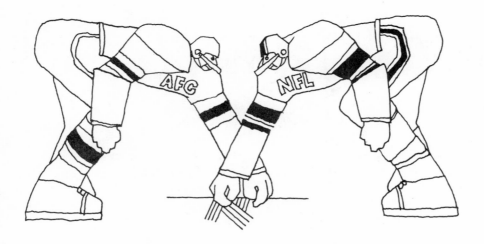

Suicide squad — A special team sent in to guard against a long kickoff return. It tries to hold the kickoff return to little or no gain.

T

Tackle — Right and left. The two players next to the guards in the offensive line. There are also two defensive tackles.

OFFENSE

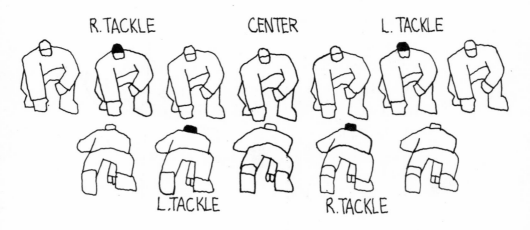

R. TACKLE　　　　CENTER　　　　L. TACKLE

L.TACKLE　　　　R.TACKLE

DEFENSE

Tackling — Stopping an opponent by tackling or blocking him to the ground.

Tee — A rubber or plastic cone used to elevate the ball on the kickoff.

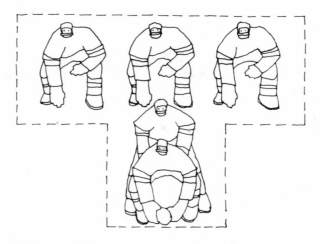

"T" formation — A popular offensive formation using either a balanced or an unbalanced line. The quarterback is positioned directly behind the center and in contact with him. The two halfbacks are about four yards behind the tackles, and the fullback is about four yards behind the quarterback to form the "T".

Take to the air — A team concentrates on a forward passing attack.

Tailback — An offensive backfield player. He is the farthest back in the backfield in a single-wing formation.

Ten-man rush — Every player on the defensive team, except for the safety, attempts to crash in on the quarterback or ball carrier.

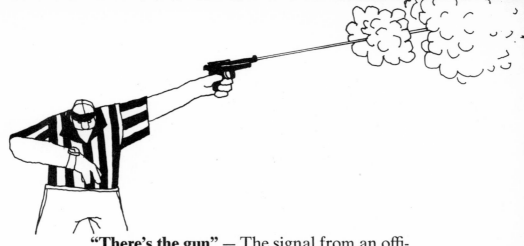

"There's the gun" — The signal from an official indicating either the end of the game or the end of the first half.

Three-pointer — A team scores three points when it kicks a field goal.

Three-point stance — A player crouches with one hand on the ground in front of him, making contact with the ground at three points, two feet and one hand.

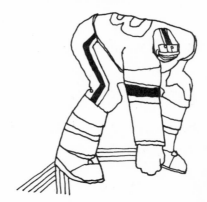

Throws a bullet — The quarterback fires a very hard straight pass.

Tight end — The offensive end who stays close to the line.

Time-out — A period of time in which the clock is stopped for reason of injury, assessing penalties, or changing linemarkers when a first down has been made. A team may also call a time-out to stop the clock.

Touchback — When the ball, in possession of a defensive player, is downed in his own end zone, it is called a touchback. The team making the touchback puts the ball in scrimmage on its own twenty-yard line.

Touchdown — A play where the ball is carried past the opponent's goal line, either by rushing or passing, scoring six points.

GOAL LINE

Triple threat — A back who can run, pass, or kick.

Tripped up — A defensive player uses his foot to trip the ball carrier. The penalty is fifteen yards.

Try for point — After a team scores a touchdown, it has an opportunity to kick a one-point goal from the two-yard line. In high school and college football, two points can be scored if the try for point is completed by a successful forward pass or by a run. There are no two-point attempts allowed in professional football.

Turning up field — When a player receives a punt or a kickoff and decides to run with the ball, he is turning up field.

Turnovers — A team loses possession of the ball by a fumble, an error, or an intercepted pass.

Two men in motion — Only one man is allowed to be in motion in the backfield before the ball is snapped. There is a five-yard penalty for having two men in motion.

Too much time in the huddle — It is illegal for a team to take too much time in the huddle before getting the play off. In high school and college football, the play must be started in twenty-five seconds. In professional football, the time allowed is thirty seconds. The penalty is five yards.

U

Umpire — The referee's chief aid, who is stationed behind the defense.

Unbalanced line — An offensive line with the majority of players on one side of the center, usually four players on one side and two on the other. The imbalance is usually made by one of the guards joining the guard on the other side of the line.

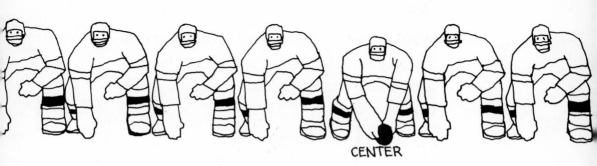

CENTER

Undershift — The defensive line or backfield players shift from a normal position to one opposite the weak side of the offensive formation.

Unnecessary roughness — A fifteen-yard penalty called by the officials under the following situations: 1. When an opponent strikes a player anywhere above the knees with the foot or any part of the leg below the knee; 2. When a player tackles the runner when he is clearly out of bounds; 3. When a player throws a runner to the ground after the ball is dead; 4. When a player runs or throws himself into or at a player who is out of the play, before or after the ball is dead; 5. When any other action is considered by the officials to be unnecessarily rough.

W

Waiting end — The defensive end waits for the play to come to him instead of charging across the scrimmage line. A waiting tackle does the same.

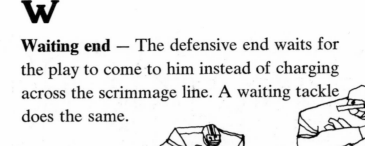

Wave system — A method of covering punts in which units of a kicking team run downfield in successive waves.

Weak side — The side of an unbalanced line containing the least number of players.

Weave — A runner dodges and twists from side to side in a zig-zag course.

Wedge — A wedge-shaped formation of interference formed by offensive blockers.

Wide — An end plays wide when he is spaced at a considerable distance from the tackle towards the sideline.

Wingback — An offensive back who lines up outside the extremity of his own line, flanking his end.

Wing "T" — The offensive linemen line up in a formation one foot apart. One halfback positions himself one yard back and outside of one of the end positions.

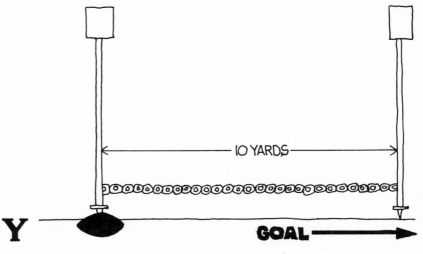

Y

Yardage chain — The yardage chain shows the players how far they must carry the ball to make a first down. The chain is ten yards long and is attached to the bottom of two rods. At the beginning of each first down, one end of the chain is placed in line with the ball. The other end is stretched the full ten yards in the direction of the goal. Every time a team makes a first down, the yardage chain is moved.

Yard line — Any line parallel to the end lines and between the sidelines.

Z

Zone defense — In defending against the pass, each defensive back guards a certain territory and defends against anyone who tries to catch a pass in his zone.

110

Greatest Players of All Time

Who were the greatest players of all time? There are many conflicting opinions, but most of the experts agree on one thing: that to be a football "great" one must succeed not only in college, but also in the tough, hard-bitten world of professional football. Many All-Americans are great stars in college, but they cannot make it in the professional leagues where the competition is harder.

In 1963, the National Football League installed the pro-football Hall of Fame in Canton, Ohio. There they have emblazoned certain names as the best football players who ever lived. The original list is called The Charter Team. First and foremost at halfback is the legendary Indian,

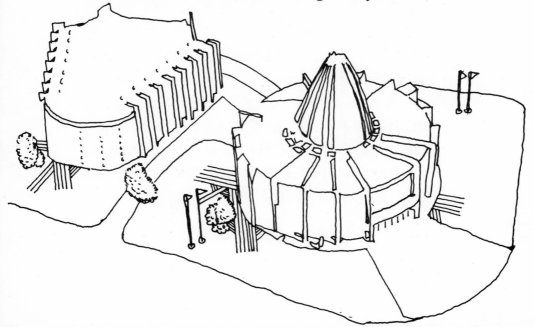

JIM THORPE

Jim Thorpe, who is considered the finest athlete of all time. In addition to his college football exploits at Carlisle, in Pennsylvania, and stardom in professional football (first with the Canton Bulldogs and later with other teams), Jim won the decathlon and many other track honors at the 1912 Olympic Games held in Stockholm, Sweden. The King of Sweden awarded Jim his medals and said, "You are the greatest athlete in the world today."

Jim also played Big League baseball with several major league teams, including the New York Giants. It is in football, however, where he is unanimously hailed as the greatest all-around player who ever lived. He could run, pass, punt, and drop-kick better than any player before or since. He possessed the deadly straight arm to

ward off tacklers, and with his tremendous blocking and whirling hips, he would leave defensive
players unconscious all over the field. He was
also a fierce tackler on the defense. In Jim's day,
team members played both offensive and defensive positions.

The other backfield "greats" selected for the
first Hall of Fame team include, Harold "Red"
Grange, who brought popularity to the professional game as a Chicago Bear. Red starred at
Illinois, where one Saturday he scored four touchdowns in twelve minutes against Michigan, a
major football power. Red, who was nicknamed
the "Galloping Ghost," was one of the most elusive, agile, tricky runners who ever put on a
football uniform.

RED GRANGE

113

Another back on the original Charter Team was the fabulous Johnny "Blood" McNally of the Green Bay Packers. He was known as the "magnificent screwball" for his antics on and off the field, but he was a tower of strength under the stress of important crises.

JOHNNY McNALLY

For fullback, Ernie Nevers, "the iron man," was the choice. The blonde destroyer from Stanford, California, could run as hard as any man, and could demolish a defensive line by pounding it time after time.

ERNIE NEVERS

Bronko Nagursky, who made all-American at Minnesota as both tackle and fullback, is considered the greatest fullback. He played that position for the Chicago Bears and was virtually unstoppable. He was a one-man gang, often dragging half the defensive team over the goal line with him. It required three or four men to slow him down and the rest of the defensive team's help to bring him to a halt.

BRONKO NAGURSKY

Dutch Clark, quarterback for the Detroit Lions, also made the Charter Team. Dutch, called the "Flying Dutchman," could do everything — run, kick, pass, and block. His talents won many games and solidified the Detroit Lions' franchise in the National Football League.

DUTCH CLARK

SAMMY BAUGH

Most experts agree that Slingin' Sammy Baugh of the Washington Redskins was the greatest passer of all time. No defense ever set up could stop the slinger from demolishing it with his lightning passes. He could peg them short or long with deadly accuracy. He brought the Redskins to the championship for many years in the NFL.

DON HUTSON

Of course, the greatest end of all time is the incomparable Don Hutson of the Green Bay Packers. He was deceptively slight, and would shuffle along in his own peculiar fashion; then suddenly he'd whip out in the clear and grab a pass for a touchdown or a long gain. The opposition always assigned two or three men to guard him, but none could stop "the Alabama Antelope."

Another great end of his era was Guy Chamberlin, who played with the Canton Bulldogs, the Cleveland Bulldogs, and many other teams, including the Chicago Cardinals.

Among the immortal linemen picked by the experts for the first Hall of Fame team was Pete "Fats" Henry, the "jolly jolter," who was one of the greatest tackles in football history. He, too, was deceptive looking. He seemed round and fat and amiable, but once the action started, he moved with amazing speed. With muscles of steel he destroyed the linemen in front of him, knocked down the interference, and nailed the runner.

PETE HENRY

119

CAL HUBBARD

Another great lineman was a giant of a tackle named Cal Hubbard. He later made a reputation as an umpire in the major leagues. Big Cal was one of the strongest men ever to play football. He starred for the New York Giants and later for the Green Bay Packers, terrorizing the opposing linemen on both offense and defense.

The center picked for the Charter Team was the indestructible Mel Hein from Washington

MEL HEIN

State and later the New York Giants. Mel was tough on both offense and defense. He roamed into his opponent's backfield, breaking up plays, messing up the interference, and in general, operating as an armored tank. Hein always played clean, but he played hard. He was a deadly tackler and could pull out of the line to lead the interference. He roved from one side of the line to the other, and anyone in his way was crushed to the ground.

Besides the all-time great players, the first Hall of Fame contains the names of these men who made outstanding contributions to professional football: Joe Carr, pioneer president of the National Football League, who guided it in its perilous early years; Bert Bell, also an NFL president, who later succeeded in solidifying the gains initially made by Joe Carr; Tim Mara, the smiling Irishman, who started the New York Giants' franchise and molded it into one of the great organizations in pro football; George Preston Marshall, an outstanding showman, who converted the unsuccessful Boston franchise into the

JOE CARR

great Washington Redskins' dynasty. He introduced the colorful half-time shows and bands which now entertain millions of fans. Last, but not least, George Halas, the "pappa bear" of the mighty Chicago Bears. He served the Bears as player, coach and owner. He forged the franchise into a powerful machine climaxed by an amazing 73-0 victory over the Washington Redskins in a league championship game.

GEORGE HALAS

Since the original Charter Team, there have been many other great players chosen for the Hall of Fame. No one can be selected for membership until five years have elapsed after his leaving the game.

Jim Brown, the Cleveland Browns' great fullback, would have dented any line that ever moved and is now in the Hall of Fame. So is Marion Motley, who was also a fullback for an earlier Cleveland Browns team. Other great players who have made the Hall of Fame since the original 1963 roster are Chuck Bednarik, a center and linebacker for the Philadelphia Eagles; Tom Fears of the Los Angeles Rams, an all-star end; Sid Luckman, a great quarterback of the Chicago Bears, who engineered the famous 73-0 victory over Washington, and was responsible for the popularity of the "T" formation; Y. A. Tittle of San Francisco and the Giants, an outstanding quarterback; Otto Graham of the Cleveland Browns; and Arnie Herber of the Green Bay Packers. Several men who are still playing will

JIM BROWN

undoubtedly be picked for the Hall of Fame five years after their careers are ended. Dick Butkus, the Chicago linebacker, is headed for immortality. So is Johnny Unitas, "Mister Quarterback," who gained glory with the Baltimore Club. Gail Sayers, who recently retired from Chicago with the reputation as one of the great runners in the game, will undoubtedly be picked in the future.

Another newly-risen star is O. J. Simpson, who recently broke Jim Brown's long-standing record by rushing over 2,000 yards in a single season. Many fans predicted that the record could never be broken.

In the years to come many other great stars will rise and shine in the gridiron heavens, but the above-mentioned athletes have proved by their feats on the ribbed gridirons that they truly deserve the epitaph of the Greatest Players That Ever Lived.

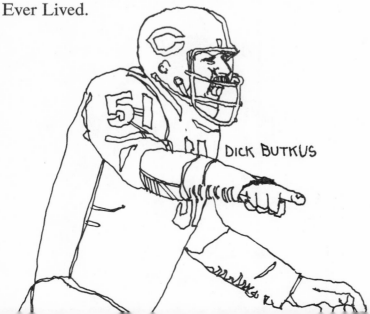

DICK BUTKUS

Larry Sutton is a young, Brooklyn-born artist and a graduate of the School of Visual Arts in New York City, where he currently resides. He has done magazine illustrations and now designs book covers. His work has appeared in New York's Washington Square Outdoor Art Exhibit for the past two years. In the *Football Dictionary*, Mr. Sutton has combined his artist's talents with his interest and participation in sports, particularly his experience as a league football player.

Joseph Olgin's new *Football Dictionary* is a reflection of his life-long love of and involvement with young people and sports. As a former player and coach, he brings a personal and practical knowledge to his writings. As a former teacher and school principal, he responds enthusiastically to the needs and interests of kids. Mr. Olgin, who lives in New Jersey, is the author of several stories and books, including *Sports Stories for Boys,* published by Harvey House. He also writes for radio and television.